For every child trying to tame an ADHD monster, and for every adult who loves them.

A NOTE ABOUT THIS BOOK:

My ADHD Monster is a children's book written to help kids who are struggling with an ADHD diagnosis. This book is NOT a diagnostic tool and no book can replace therapy or medical opinion.

If you are seeking information on next steps for your child, you can visit my website at chivaunoldes.com and check out the resources tab for links to help.

This is my monster. He lives in my brain and makes it work differently.

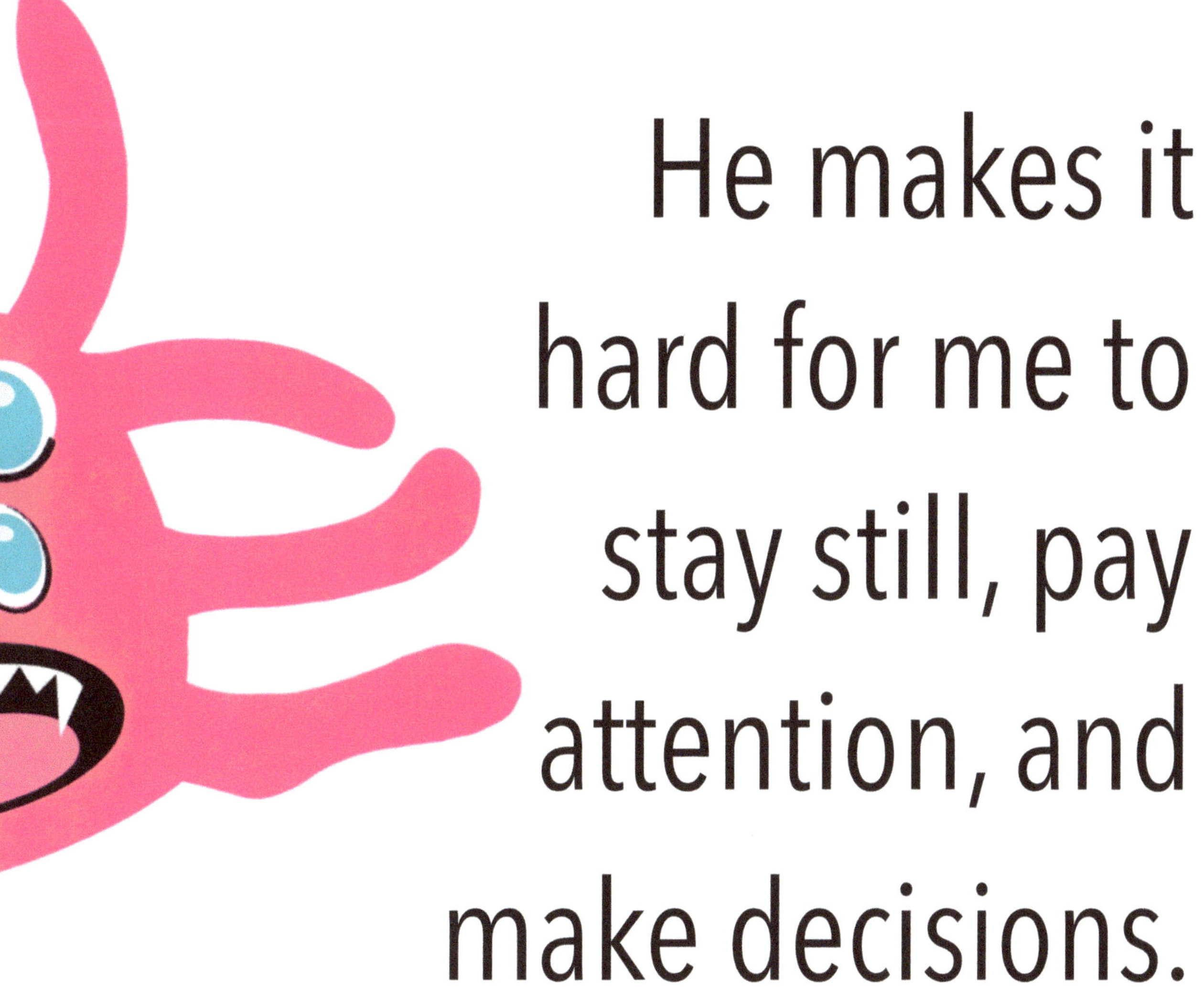

He makes it hard for me to stay still, pay attention, and make decisions.

Blah, blah, blah, blah...

Sometimes my monster is so loud that he makes all the other sounds confusing and uncomfortable.

He makes my mind spin so fast that I forget what I am supposed to be doing. Sometimes I even get in trouble for not listening.

Sometimes he makes me feel so jumpy and over-excited ...

that I find it hard
to be still.

He really likes to make big messes and put things where they don’t belong so that I can’t find them when I need them.

He makes my feelings go up and down like a roller coaster so that I feel very emotional.

I talk to the grown-ups in my life and together we work to tame my monster and keep him calm.

I talk to a therapist. She is like a doctor for my brain. We name my monster ADHD. That stands for Attention Deficit Hyperactivity Disorder.

Rx

We make a plan for taming my monster. We also decide if I should take medicine to help him stay quiet and focused during school.

Being organized and making a daily routine with my family helps me to stay on task and remember what I should be doing.

My teacher, parents, and therapist work together to help me do well in school when I might need extra help or a place to calm down.

When my monster makes me wiggly and restless, I use my recess and after school time to get my energy out through play.

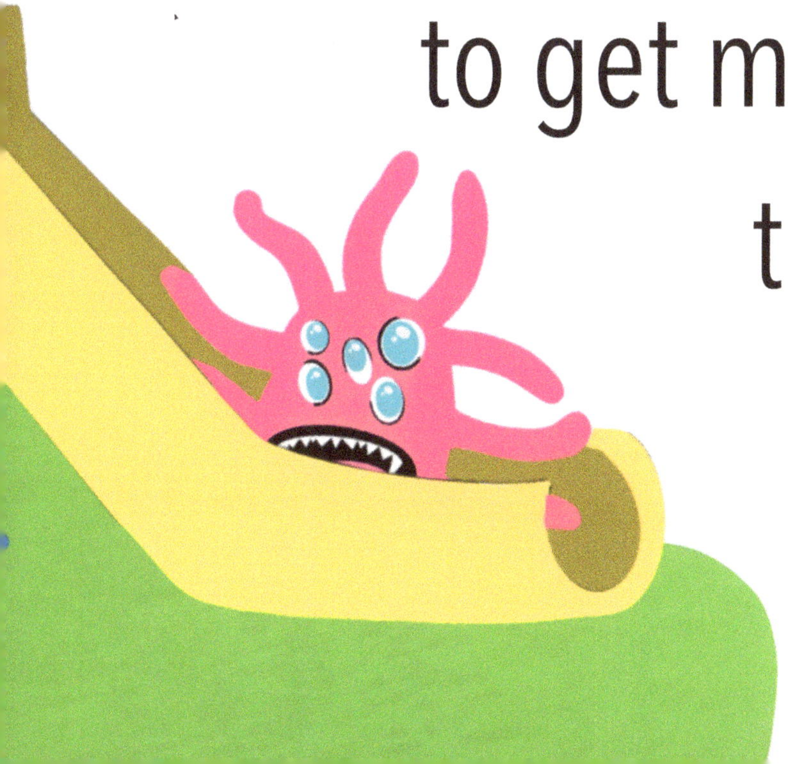

If I am somewhere that I cannot run or play, I bring fidget toys with me to keep my hands busy and my monster focused.

When my feelings get too big and loud, I take a deep breath and count backwards from 10.

When I feel calm I can tell someone how I am feeling and what I need.

Having an ADHD monster is hard sometimes. It can make me feel different and lonely.

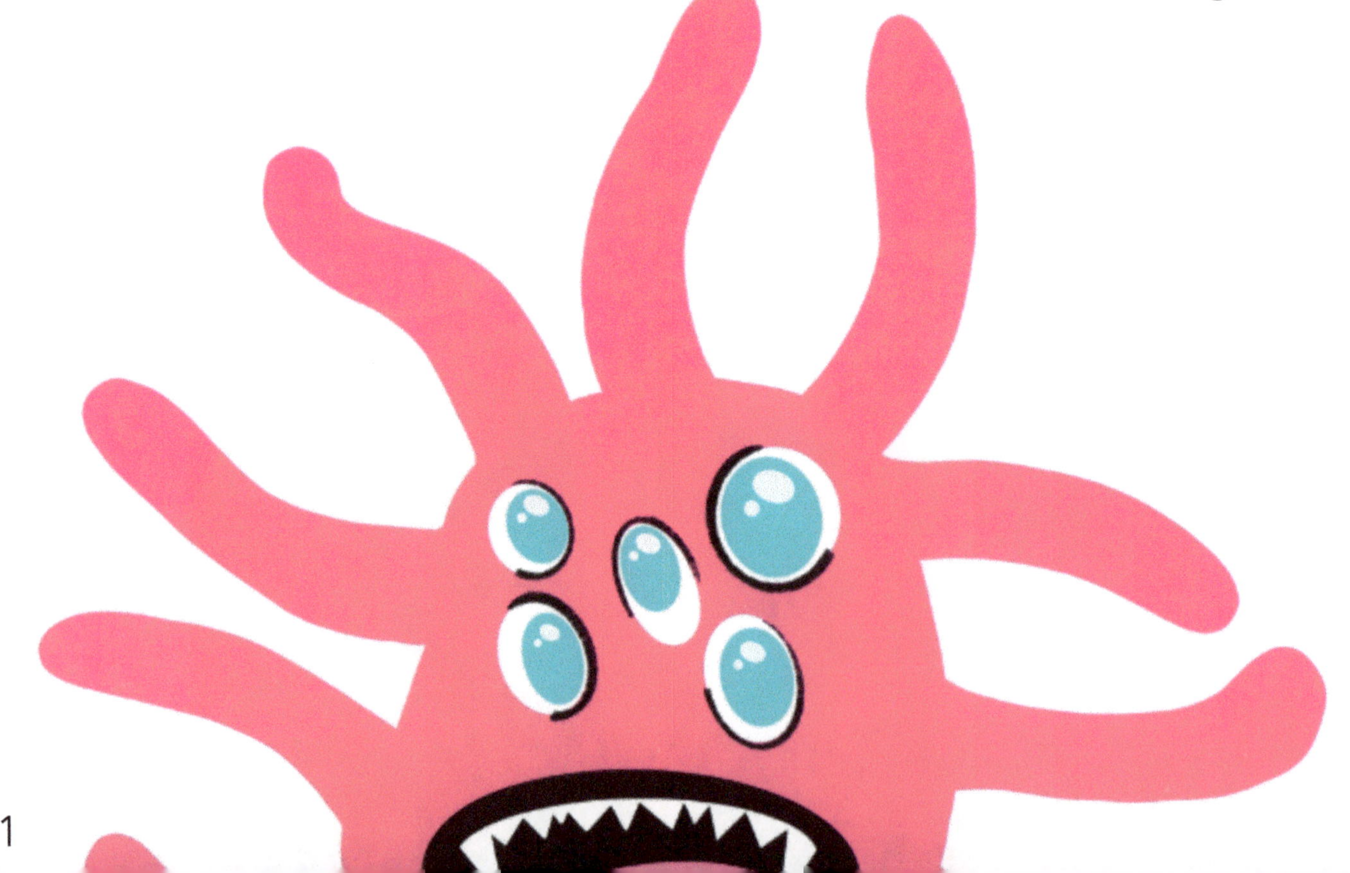

But my monster also makes me feel special. He helps me to imagine, create, and dream up things that nobody else can.

My monster is a part of me, so I guess he must be pretty special too.

www.ingramcontent.com/pod-product-compliance
Lightning Source LLC
Chambersburg PA
CBHW041821110726
48006CB00019B/2456

* 9 7 9 8 2 1 8 2 3 3 0 9 9 *